PHOTO
ENTOURAGE

PHOTO ENTOURAGE

A Tracing File Sourcebook

ERNEST BURDEN

McGraw-Hill, Inc.

New York St. Louis San Francisco Auckland Bogota
Caracas Hamburg Lisbon London Madrid Mexico
Milan Montreal New Delhi Paris
San Juan São Paulo Singapore
Sydney Tokyo Toronto

Library of Congress Cataloging-in-Publication Data

Burden, Ernest E., date.
    Photo entourage : a tracing file sourcebook / Ernest Burden.
        p.   cm.
    ISBN 0-07-008936-1
    1. Entourage (Architectural drawing)   2. Photography — Reproduction
of plans, drawings, etc.   I. Title.
    NA2780.B874   1990
    720'.28'4 — dc20   90-13410
                                                                                CIP

Acknowledgment

This book represents a unique combination of artistic,
photographic, and reproduction techniques. I am
indebted to those people who assisted in these efforts
to make this book an outstanding technical
achievement.

Designed by Ernest Burden

CONTENTS

FIGURES

Stylish 2
Minorities 12
Casual Attire 16
Groups 32
Back Views 40
Families 44
Bicycles 57
Walking Dogs 67
Photographers 71
Police 75
Seated 77
Aerial Views 83
Handicapped 92

VEHICLES

Oblique Views 98
Front And Back Views 103
Rotational Views 103
Aerial Views 118
Prototype Models 129
Fire/Rescue 135
Emergency Services 138

BOATS

Marina And Harbor 140
Dockside 143
Marina 146
Aerial Views 151
Airplanes/Ground 155
Airplanes/Air 156

PLANTS

Tropical 158
Ferns 160
Indoor Lobbies 165
Planters 167
Potted 168
Greenhouse 171
Hanging Pots 173

TREES

Branches 176
Trunks 179
Winter Outline 183
Ornamental 191
Snow Covered 192
Night Lights 195
Flowering 197
With Leaves 198
Unusual Outline 205
Looking up/Plans 209
Palms 210
Evergreens 216

ENVIRONMENT

Outdoor Plaza 222
Mall Escalators 224
Flags 227
Parade 229
Fountains 231
Sculpture 232
Paving Patterns 233
Aerial Views 237
Clouds 245
Fireworks 247

PREFACE

When ENTOURAGE: A Tracing File was published almost a decade ago, it was the first time that images designed specifically to enhance architectural drawings were assembled into book form. Although the drawings in that book were all derived from photographs, they were reproduced as line drawings that had been traced over these photographs. The drawings were executed by several artists and architectural illustrators, including many drawn by the author. As with all tracing portfolios, the success of the drawing depends on the talent of the artist interpreting the photograph. Fortunately, the talents of those represented in that book were of the highest caliber, and reflected the depth of experience in architectural renditions.

PHOTO-ENTOURAGE goes to the source. It presents photographs of the actual subject in the highest quality reproduction. This allows you to create your own tracing file, using your own drawing techniques.

Thousands of photographs were taken by the author for the preparation of the original tracing files. Several thousand more were taken for this book from countless sources and locations. People were photographed in many different situations in many parts of the country, from the high-style annual Easter parade on Fifth Avenue in New York City, to the relaxed atmosphere of resorts.

The trees were photographed across the country to represent many species in all seasons. Automobiles were photographed at current expositions, and features experimental and prototype models as well as current models. They are all presented in rotational viewpoints to fit most any perspective angle. The distracting backgrounds have been opaqued out for ease of tracing. This is not necessary for the trees, or for the people However, the figures were enhanced by eliminating certain background elements, such as signs and other clutter, so the image presented is the easiest to convert to drawings.

The book is designed to open flat for easy tracing, or the pages can be taken out of the book for making enlargements or reductions. Most "clip art" books or tracing files take up valuable room with several sizes of the same image The office copiers of today make this unnecessary. With 1% increments, you have access to endless economical variations of each image in this book. By copying the images onto acetate, or vellum, you can obtain a reverse image by simply turning over the transparent sheet. When tracing the images, a matte acetate works best, using a narrow pen such as a 0.25 width or smaller. Once the image is traced onto acetate it can also be used in the mirror image by simply turning over the sheet. Some images can be photocopied directly as high-contrast images, such as the winter outline trees, and the results will be close to that of a drawing.

In addition to enlarging or reducing the images by photocopying, they can be digitized into a computer, and manipulated with various software programs. The high-quality photographs were printed using a fine-line screen to preserve as much of the detail as possible. Scanning the images can be done using a variety of methods, including hand scanners. The images can then be made into line art, various gray-scale renditions, or posterized into a graphic image.

Certain programs can enhance the drawing through functions like the "auto-trace", which literally automatically traces the outline of the figure, converting it into a line drawing. Additional features of certain software programs are the capability to stretch or shrink the image on one axis only, making thin figures out of heavy ones, or tall trees out of short ones. The format of this book is much like a portfolio wherein each page, front and back, has the identical subject matter. They can be removed and placed in a filing system of your own, either in a folder, or a three ring binder. The pages were designed with enough room to accommodate the three-hole punch.

Every effort has been taken to provide you with the most usable images to trace. The subjects were carefully selected for their use in architectural illustrations. The size of the images makes them easy to trace directly. The backgrounds were eliminated and enhanced to provide a clear image to trace. The high quality reproduction makes them suitable for enlargements to any size. The entire book was produced to create the best possible images for you to use in creating your own photographically accurate, and professional quality tracing file.

The rest is up to you.

FIGURES

Stylish
Minorities
Casual Attire
Groups
Back Views
Families
Bicycles
Walking Dogs
Photographers
Police
Seated
Aerial Views
Handicapped

2 FIGURES: Stylish

FIGURES: Stylish 3

4 FIGURES: Stylish

6 FIGURES: Stylish

8 FIGURES: Stylish

12 FIGURES: Minorities

14 FIGURES: Costume Dress

16 FIGURES: Casual Attire

18 FIGURES: Casual Attire

20 FIGURES: Couples

22 FIGURES: Couples

24 FIGURES: Street Attire

26 FIGURES: Street Attire

28 FIGURES: Street Attire

30 FIGURES: Casual Attire

32 FIGURES: Street Groups

34 FIGURES: Casual Groups

36 FIGURES: Casual Groups

40 FIGURES: Backs

42 FIGURES: Backs

46 FIGURES: Families

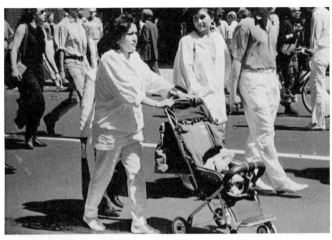

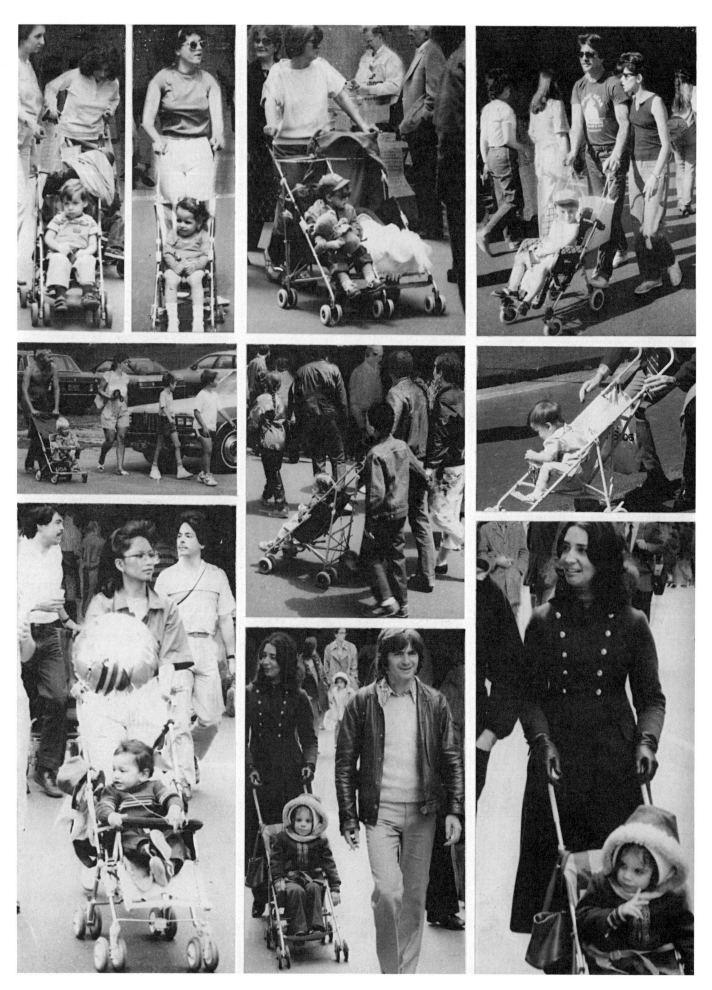

50 FIGURES: Families

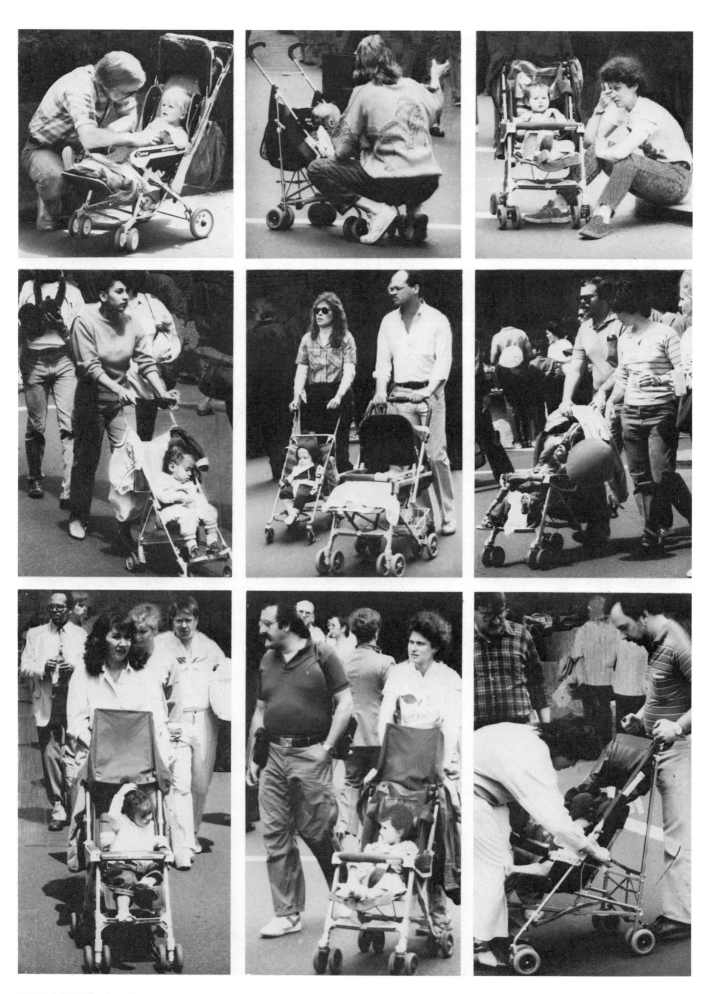

52 FIGURES: Families

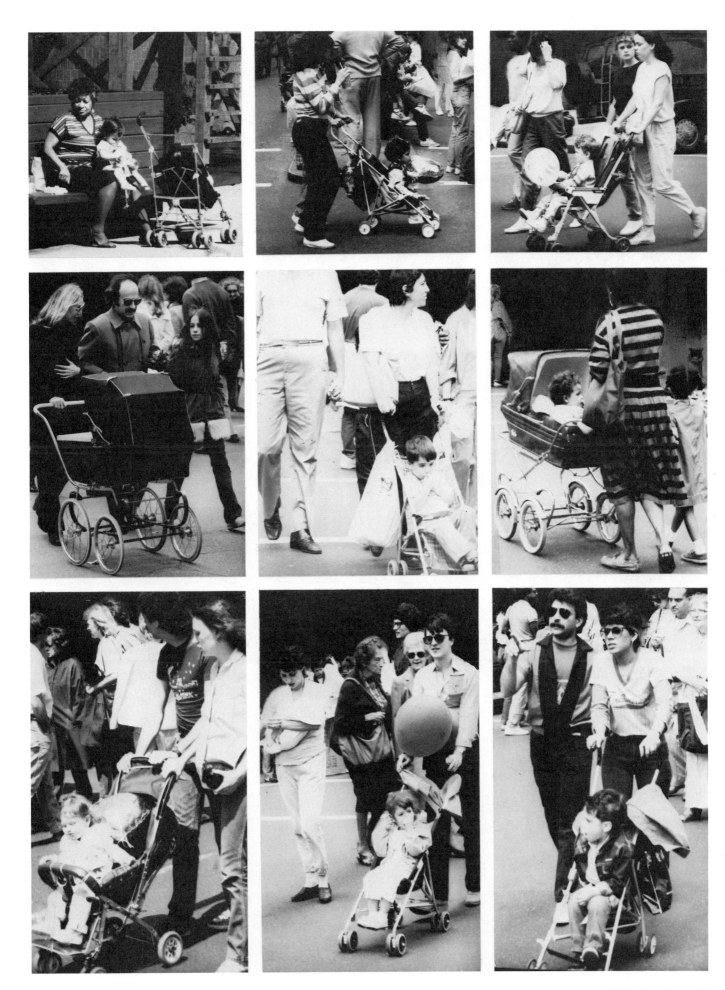

54 FIGURES: Families

58 FIGURES: Bicycles

60 FIGURES: Bicycles

68 FIGURES: With Dogs

72 FIGURES: Photographers

74 FIGURES: Hailing Cabs

76 FIGURES: Police On Horseback

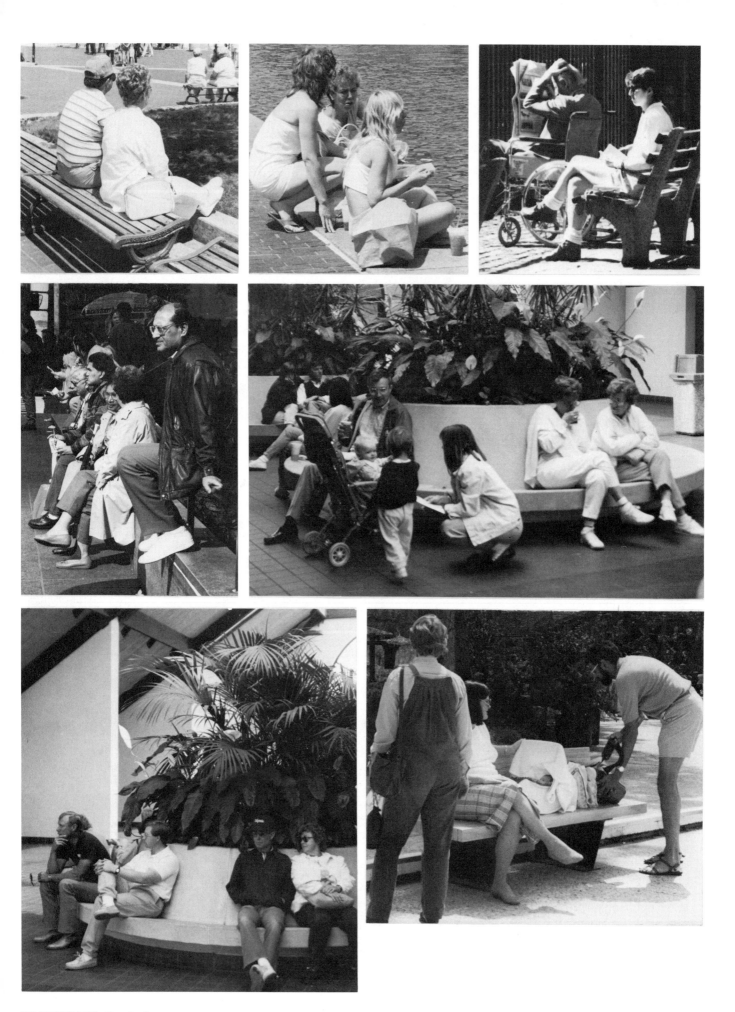

82 FIGURES: Outdoor Cafe

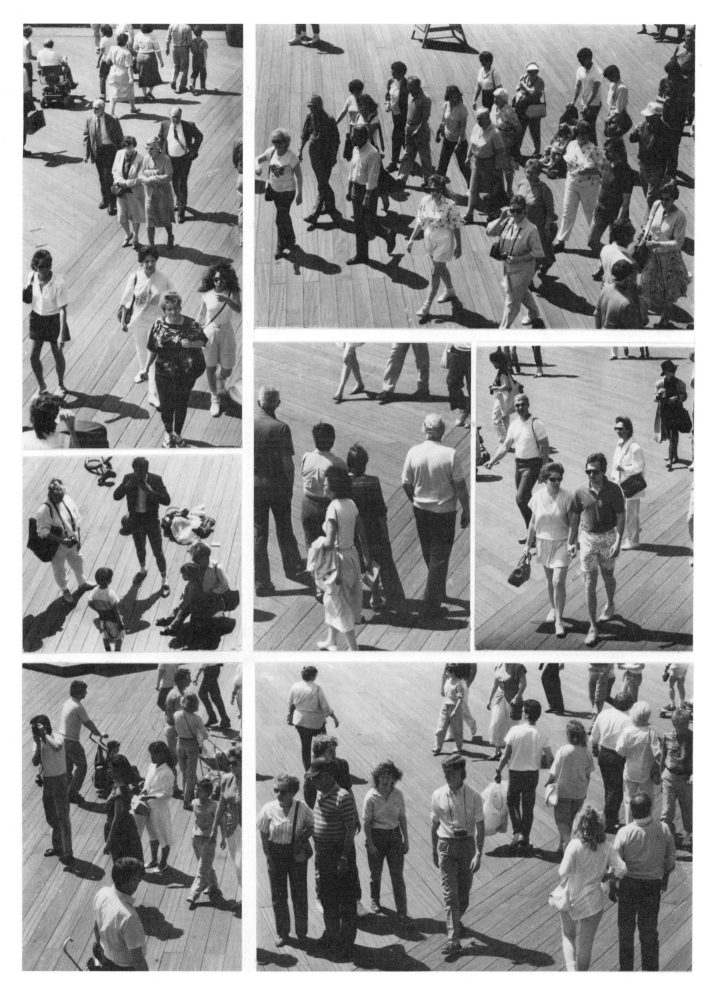

84 FIGURES: Aerial Views

86 FIGURES: Aerial Views

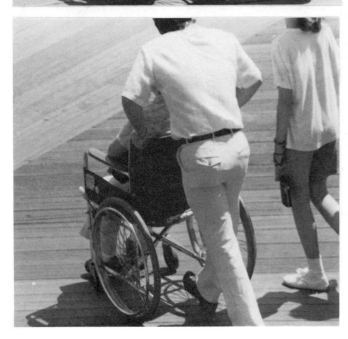

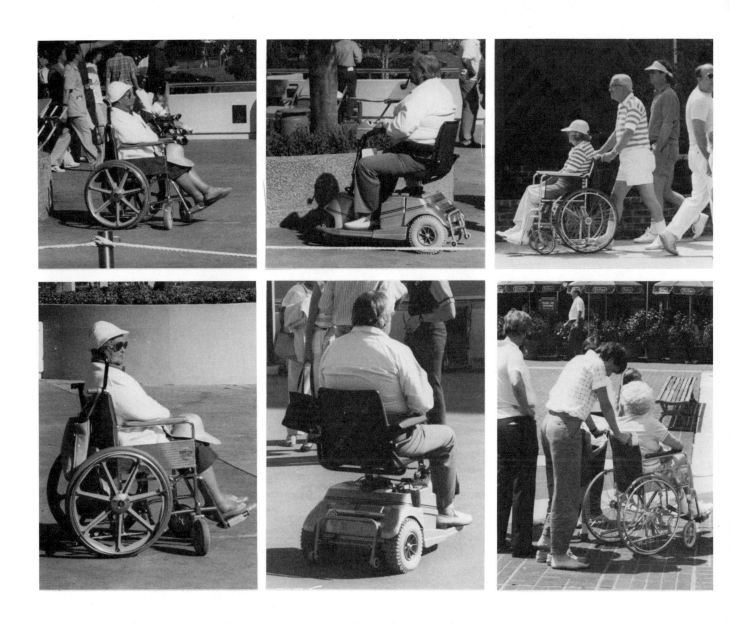

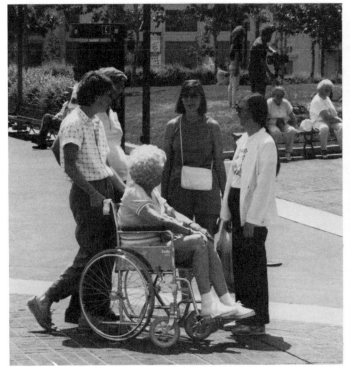

96 FIGURES: Handicapped

VEHICLES

Oblique Views
Front and Back Views
Rotational Views
Prototype Models
Emergency Services

98 VEHICLES: Oblique Views

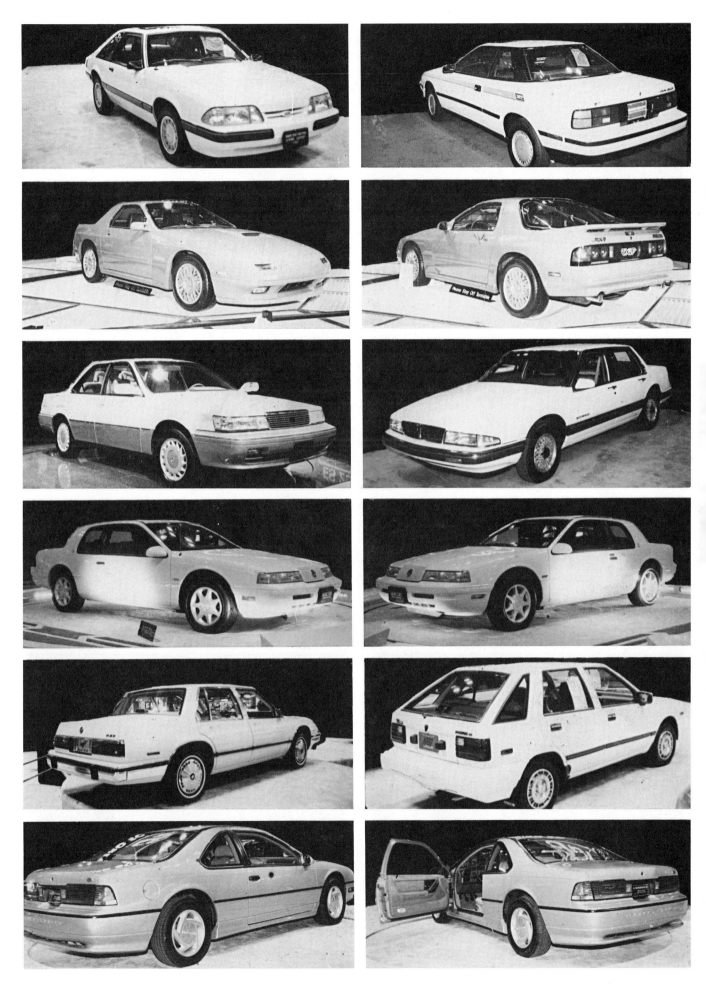

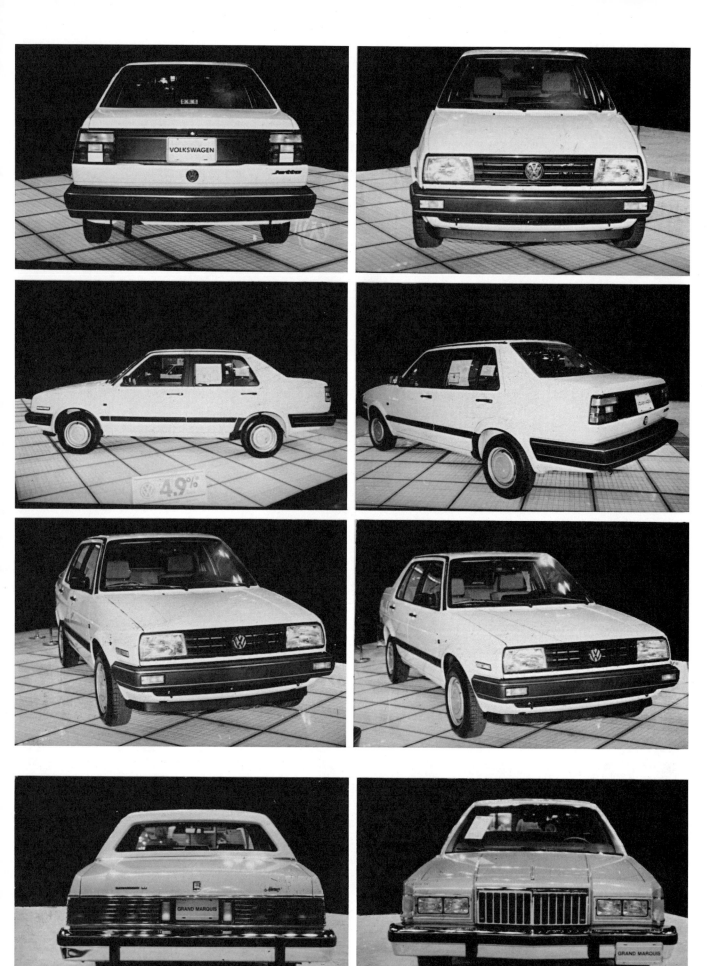

100 VEHICLES: Oblique Views

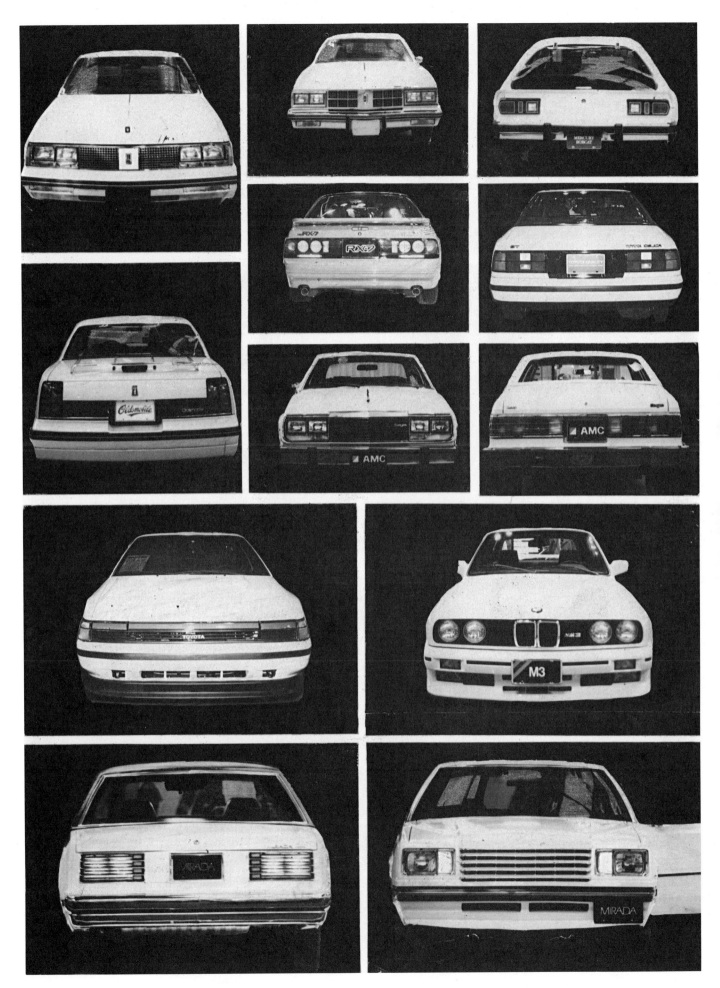

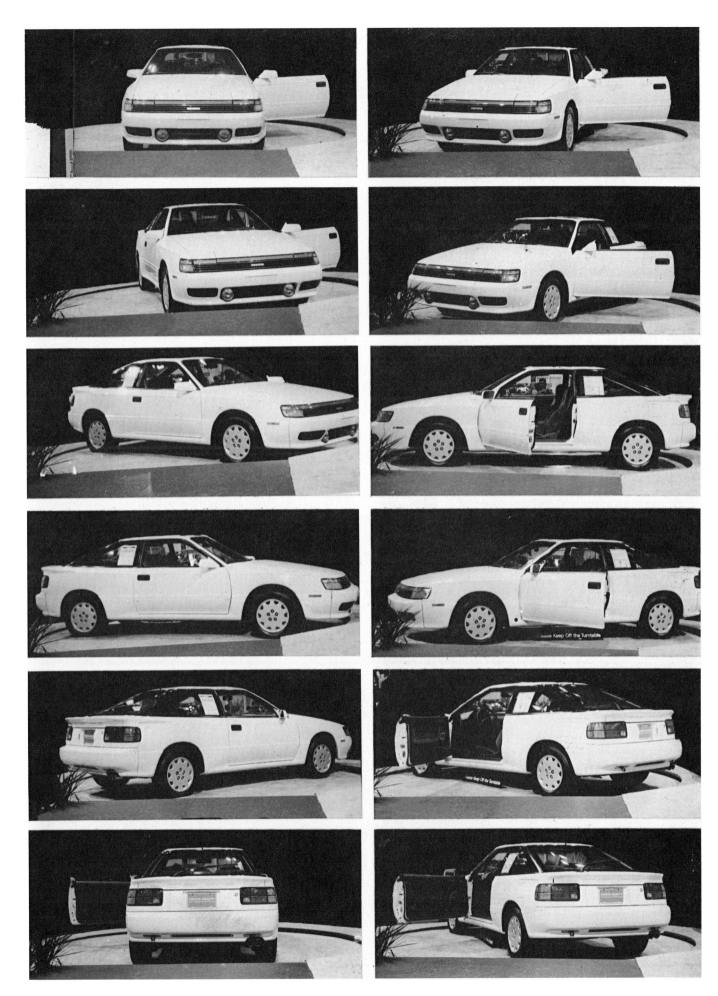

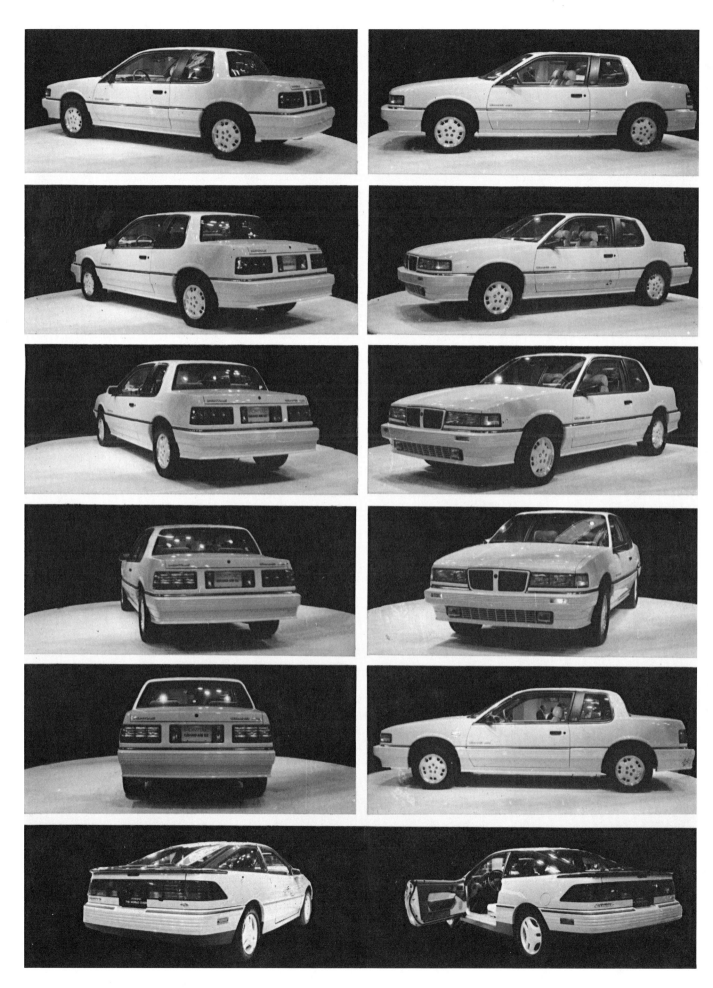

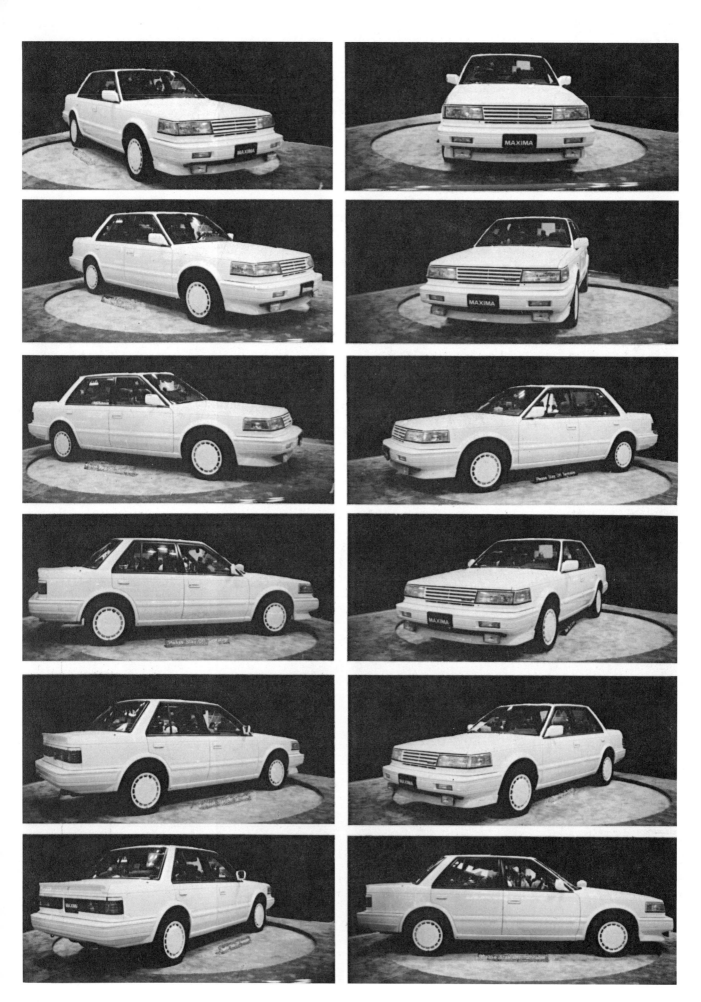

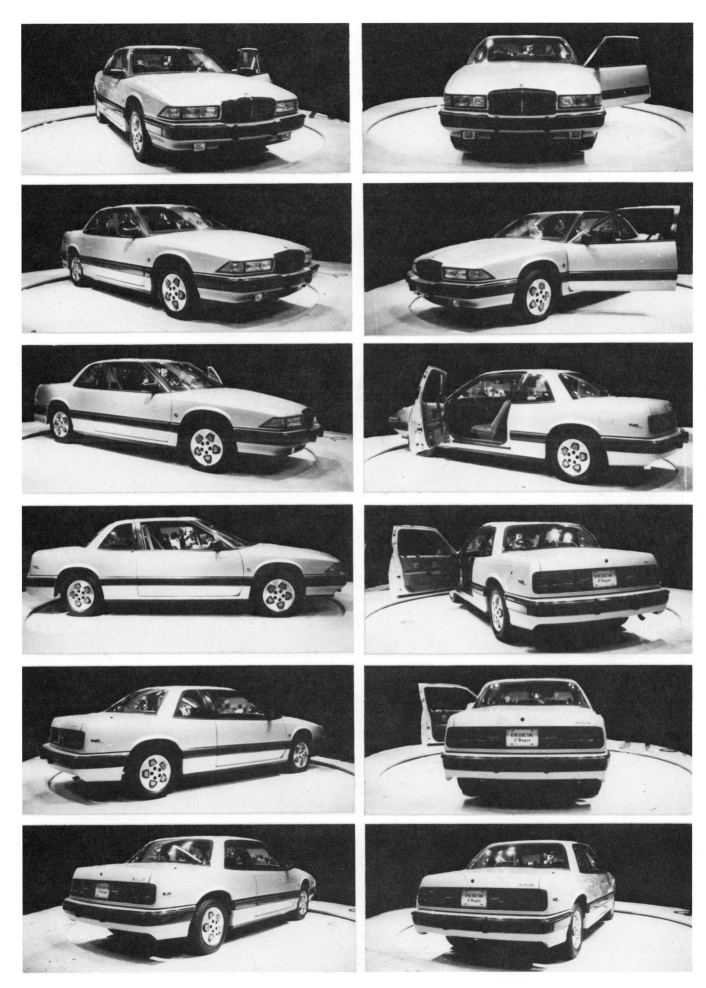

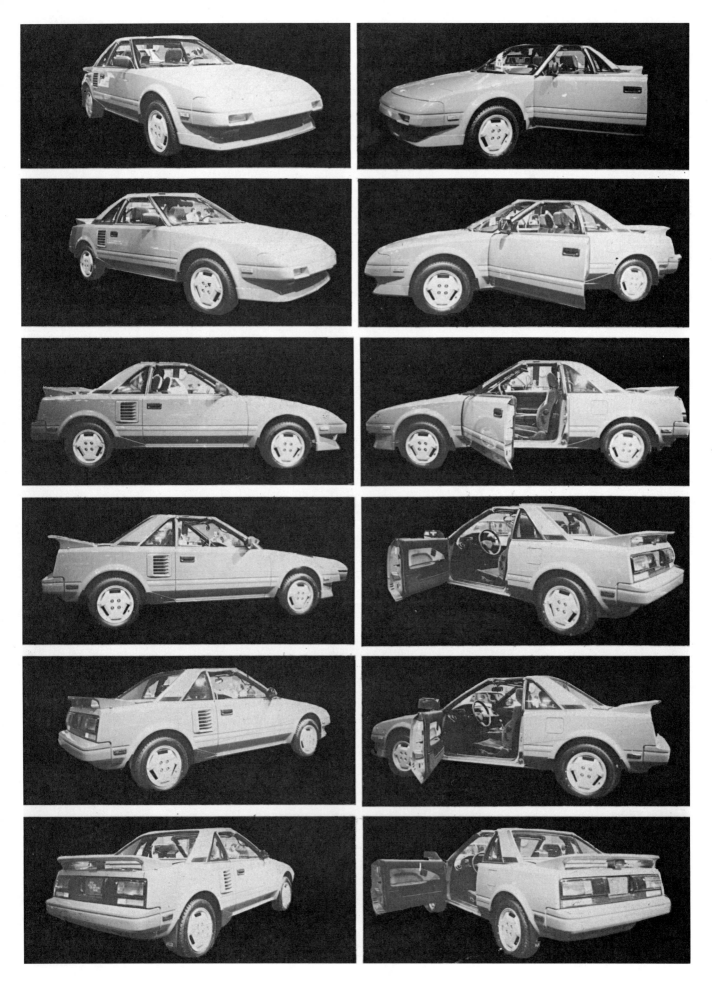

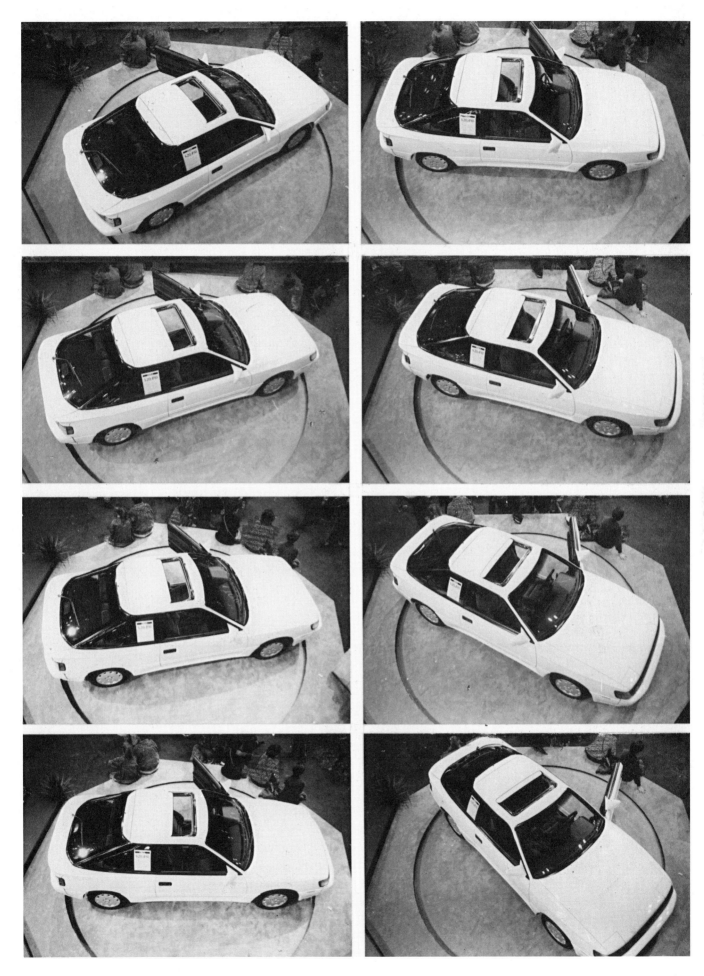

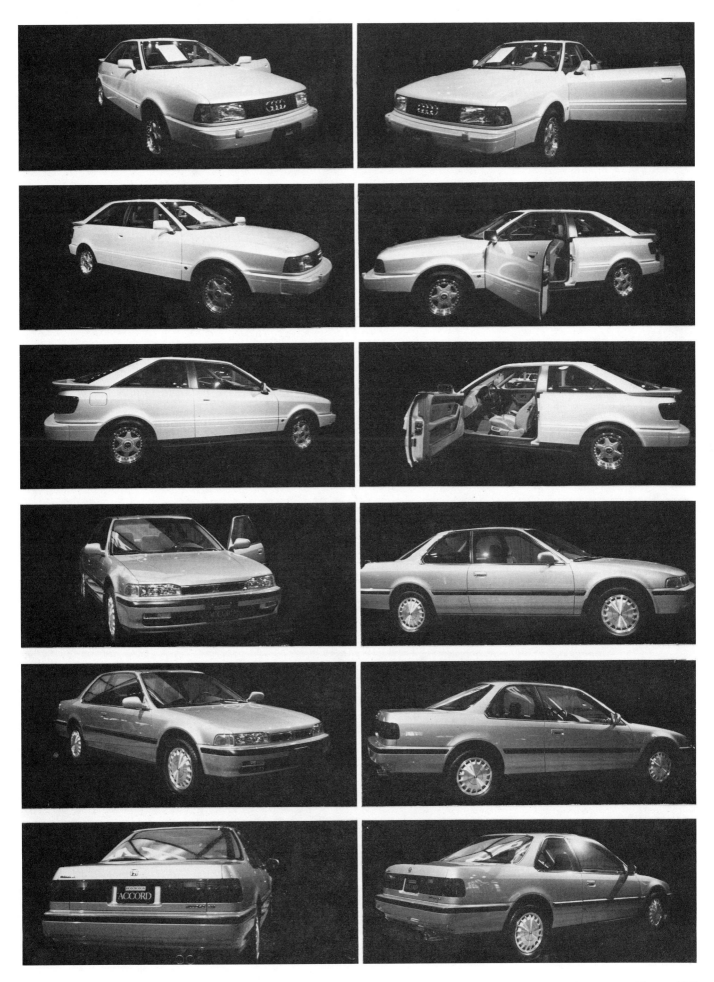

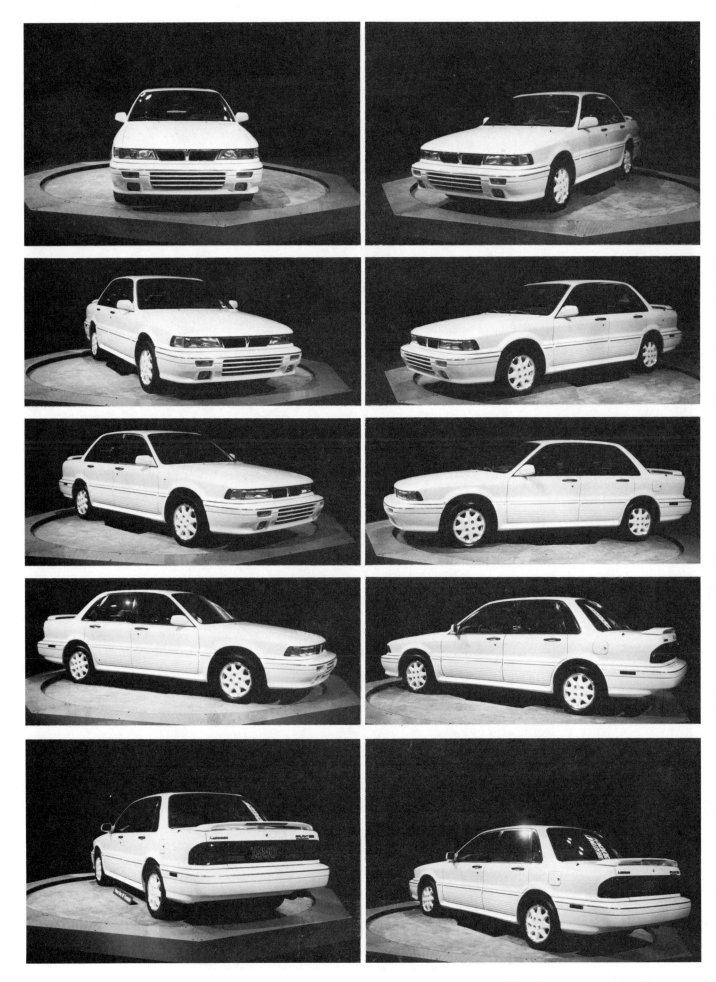

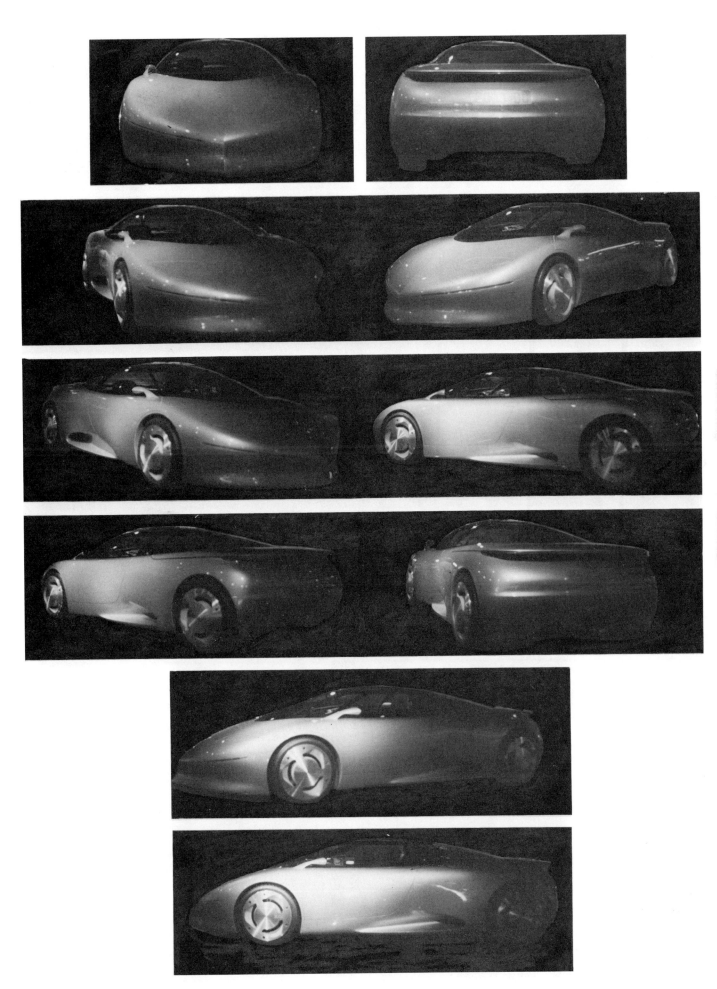

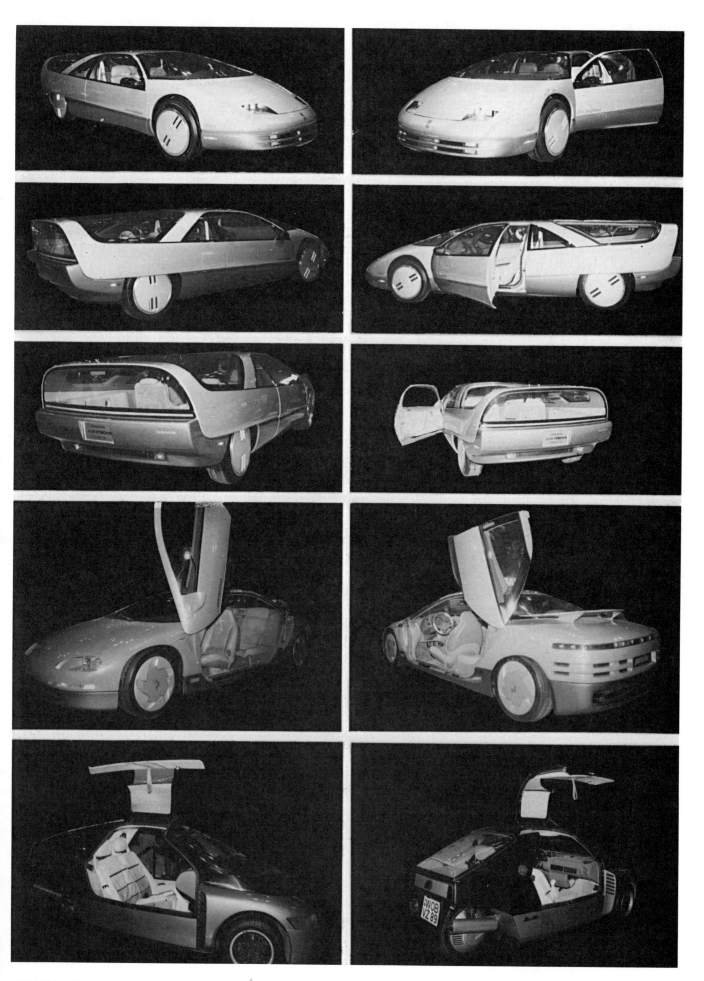

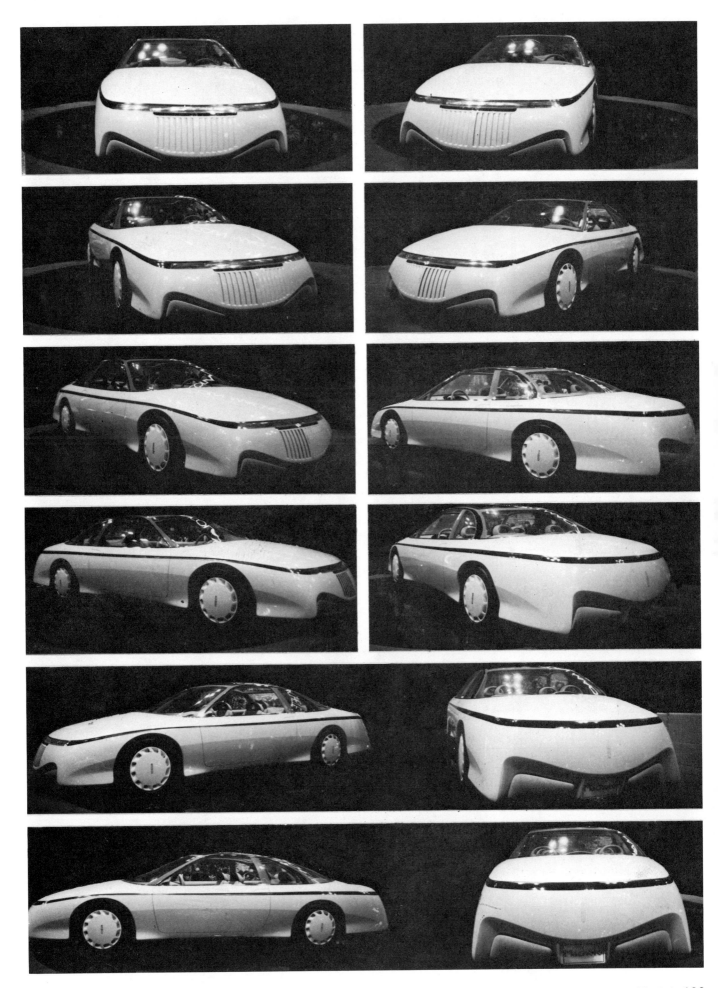

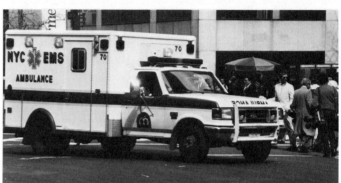

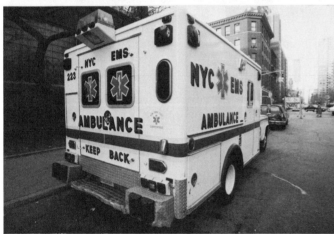

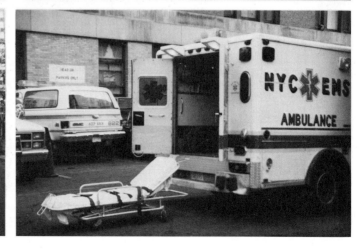

BOATS

Marina and Harbor
Dockside
Aerial Views
Airplanes/Ground
Airplanes/Air

140 BOATS: Marina and Harbor

142 BOATS: Marina and Harbor

PLANTS

Tropical
Ferns
Lobbies
Planted
Potted
Greenhouse
Hanging Pots

158 PLANTS: Tropical

TREES

Branches
Trunks
Winter Outline
Ornamental
Snow Covered
Night Lights
Flowering
With Leaves
Unusual Outlines
Looking Up/Plans
Palms
Evergreens

176 TREES: Branches

186 TREES: Winter Outline

188 TREES: Winter Outline

192 TREES: Snow Covered

194 TREES: Snow Covered

198 TREES: With Leaves

200 TREES: With Leaves

204 TREES: With Leaves

206 TREES: Unusual Outline

214 TREES: Palms

ENVIRONMENT

Outdoor Plaza
Mall Escalators
Flags
Parade
Fountains
Sculpture
Paving Patterns
Rural Aerials
Suburban Aerials
Urban Center
Urban Park
Clouds
Fireworks

234 ENVIRONMENT: Paving Patterns

ENVIRONMENT: Suburban Block 239

240 ENVIRONMENT: Urban Center

244 ENVIRONMENT: Cemetary Landscape Aerials

246 ENVIRONMENT: Clouds